In Motion

Áine Maher

Est. 2021

“do you still write?”

I nod.

“have you sent anything in to be published?”

“Not yet.”

…

“Why not? There’s nothing stopping you.”

- *A conversation with my mother.*

Before you read…

This is just a little disclaimer- every piece of poetry in this book has a story to tell… many of which are personal to me. However, some of them may not have an experience from my life entwined within them. They may just express a feeling or share a story that may mean something important for another person.

For you.

But that's the beauty of poetry; where a piece has the potential to mean a million different things, for many different people. Whether that be their own personal struggles, a journey they have been on (or still on), a beloved friend… the possibilities are endless.

This book was an opportunity where I could give myself the stage, to open up and speak about a variety of topics that matter to me, and I cannot thank you enough for taking your time to read "In Motion", for whatever reason you were drawn to it.

I hope it was able to bring you comfort and security. Thank you again my lovely,
Áine xxx

P.S. nice to finally meet you!

Contents

My Head.

My Jaw.

My Body.

My Shoulders.

My Heart.

"There's a lot going on inside.
Different signals,
often trying to send the same message.
There isn't always a dead end,
but this darkness…
I'm hesitant to venture into."

-My head.

Things that went through my head after it was over.

It was almost like I could see myself outside
my body.

I was still unsure of what will become of me.
I was hungry, yet food was undesirable.
Thoughts on replay, but sleep wasn't being
chased somehow.

I felt this chill that would never go away.
A cold hand that was firmly pressed on my
shoulder.
Freezing.

I was always freezing.

This anxiousness was not friendly,
and followed me around like a lost dog.
I didn't want to be its newly found owner.
Those messages were not ideal,
some meant well,
but didn't need to know the details.

(in my therapy session).

"will I ever get over this feeling?"
"yes," my therapist said. ***"I'm here to help
you."***

That feeling would leave eventually,
but will leave a print behind,
and it may drop by every now and then,
as if to say “hello, remember me?”

“will I ever get through this?”
“Yes.” She said.

She kept that promise.

Glass Eyes

In those bright blue orbs,
I see her passions descend from her mind,
to her mouth and fingers
like a silken drape.

How strong her love for all things living,
breathing,
She cares, laughs, and comforts,
Never do I feel a nuisance in her company.

Yet,
When she mourns, her heart is angered,
even when it's broken.

Her mind tormented by the demons,
her worries flared within those eyes.

Never seen such pain,
In a sky that remains
It isn't tinted grey
when the rain decides to fall.

Instead, those eyes so blue,
they glisten like
glass.

I’m trying
to make peace
prevail.

I’m trying
to let peace
prosper.

Even though-

Through trying,
I’m only getting myself
hurt in the process,
believing that I can fix glass,
that has been smashed into a million pieces.

- It only leaves me broken too.

I sleep with my earphones in.

not
to drown out the silence itself.

But
in preparation to drown out
the darker thoughts inside my head
the overthinking,
the fear of what can happen
will happen.

I drown it out with music and stories
to wear out my brain,
and let me
finally
rest.

Away from Home.

“I want someone to hold me.
I have them in my life,
but they’re not with me,
in this current moment.
This is where I realise that I take
that warmth and comfort
for granted.”

Feelings

This dark cloud isn't consistent.
I have those days where I feel so exhausted
and
defeated.

And other days I am ready to take on anything.
those are the good days
the very ones I feel
that I own this life I was graced with.

Until reality hits me in the face,
and reminds me how quick it can make me feel
otherwise.

Thinking about loved ones:
friends,
family.
sometimes even strangers,
who had passed before their time…
has my heart-breaking piece by piece.
I always ask myself-

“what could have been done differently?”

Open your eyes.

I see a:
Damaged heart
A problem after problem
Anger
Pain
Sad
Lonely
Anxious heap of
Worthless ***exhaustion.***

Open my eyes.

We see a:
Beautiful,
Motivating,
Woman with a-
Kind
Funny,
Loving,
Protective,
Caring ***heart***

Stillness

Dead, dark, and blind,
I lie in the desolate cot like any other night.
Soft hums of the midnight travellers,
I lay, awake to their song.

When I hear no more,
I try to rest my weary eyes,
The electronic virus,
A burden that shortened my time for rest…

I am suddenly stuck,
Frozen in this time frame,
over a little thought,
A series of shakes and shivers,
I remained on my back, and stare.

The ceiling is over-shadowed,
with the creatures of the night,
they crawl, they climb, they grin…
almost wickedly it seems,
they hover, they hang,
singing, whispering,
a cold breeze along my neck…

I awake once more.
The sun light kisses the glazed windows,
As I sigh with relief at its arrival.

The demons have gone to sleep.

Countdown

The wick is running out.

This room is getting darker now.

The light has been flickering for sometime
as if to bid me time to get more light,
more sense.

a ticking of a clock,
a flicker,
a shaky breath.

There's a knock at the door,
A whisper, a shadow
Begging to let them back in.
Watching and waiting for the exact moment
to pounce.

"I'm sleeping on a dark cloud".

In this unconscious state,
Where I don't feel anyone's presence.

I never feel a hand holding mine

Or arms around me like that warm blanket
I need on the colder nights

I feel furthest away from any-
No.

Everyone.

Drifting

Swimming through space and
time.

searching, pondering and
yearning.

Waiting for you to reach back.

But alas,
I continue to float.

Missing

Have you seen this girl?

Wearing her favourite pink jumper,
black leggings,
headphones are forever stuck to her ears?

Last seen with a wide smile,
that wasn't stitched onto her face.
The passion for writing always burning,
always willing,
trying,
reliable.

She's "here" …
yet she isn't.

I'm not too sure where she went.

I want to wake up somewhere forward in time,
and skip all the mayhem.

I want to know that I'm wide awake,
in the new now,
And fast forward past the unknown,
the worry,
the disappointment
the hopelessness
of going through it all again.

-Lockdown 2021.

-Running Away-

From the chaos of life.

I'm doing all I can do,
to keep the beast happy.
There is nothing beautiful
about the status quo.

You try to keep them happy.
But it's kicked back in your face.

Why bother trying?

I may never know what truly goes on inside your head.

I hate that.
Please let me in.
Open the door.

Let's talk it out.

Gone

It breaks my heart,
to realise that
sometimes
our memories of loved ones
isn’t always about the good times.

It isn’t always about the laughter
that was shared,
the memories made
or the words spoken.

It’s often how they left us,
that overshadows
everything else.

Truth

Speak your truth,
even if starts out as a whisper.

Sing your truth,
Even if it starts out as single note.

Show your truth,
The first step is the most important.

Paint your truth,
with all the beautiful colours
that describe your mission,
                    your very existence.

Whatever way you can,
Don't let yourself
          be silenced.

You let your thoughts stack up like
dishes by the kitchen sink.
And it can be too much at times, I get
that.

But make time to declutter, wash, rinse
and organise.

So they can be put away.

-you think clearer in bigger spaces-

Year after year,
I always think of what you could be doing with your life.

Or I would think about your presence:

To hear your voice, to see a smile reach ear to ear, in person.

And not from a photograph.

I am forever thinking.

The Room with the Blue Curtains

There are many of these mysterious rooms.

In here you will find
the curtains,
closed shut and tight,
No light can squeeze through them.

A silhouette attempts to open the curtains.

But those little hands are unable to reach them.

Voices and sounds surround everything
behind these curtains,
usually things no one outside knows about.

It forces out a light flicker,
a laugh, a smile, a joke.
And tries to look for the golden light,
that can lovingly fill up the room.
...
Unfortunately,
We may never know what goes on behind
these
blue curtains,
until we find ourselves discovering,
that our brightest stars,
are bravely trying to get out...

Only to battle with the storm.

My feet may touch the ground,
but my head isn't always anchored in the same way.

Head in the clouds (i).

Wish all you like.

What you've done or said in the past
cannot be changed.

You can look back at your sixteen-year-old
self.
and think about what you would say about that
boy
or that girl,
those last words,
that decision.

But you can't change anything,
you'll only be left behind.

behind the glass wall of **now,**
of what has been done.

What you can do,
is reflect and maybe heed warning
to someone else,
so the same mistake isn't made again.

"The Fog Outside my window"

It's been around- stuck around, the last couple
days.
A thick, grey curtain.

Few souls have bravely ventured out-
I hope they found their way home again.
Safely.

Are you afraid to follow?
In fear you will not return?

I'm not; however-
I am still unsure,
where I'll end up,
walking aimlessly,
with no real purpose,
a chance my destination has not been decided
for me yet.

"Catoptric Tristesse" (n.)

You could give me all the evidence in the
world-
shower me in love,
compliments,
and even simply request my company.

I may feel this high for a while;
that buzz that keeps me talking,
                                        laughing,
up on this cloud that brings me nothing but
happiness-
the joy of your presence.

However, when that buzz wears off, I fall back
into my corner.

I want to believe you,
but sometimes feel like it isn't true,
almost like you've gotten good at hiding what
you really think of me…

Locked away,
out of my reach,
out of sight, but not out of my mind.

I'm sorry.

"Strange how you see a smile, and that's all
you can, or choose to see.

Not the thousands of dark skies,
overthinking anguish: the bashing, the torture,
and self-inflicted punishments,
that had the person stitch on the smile
in
the
first
place."

12

Hiding under the covers will not save you,
from what goes on in the now.

You become aware of what battles
people have faced without your knowledge.

Secrets that uncover themselves,
ones that you never wanted to know.
Pain and heartache
you would wish you had never experienced.

Please, I beg you,
do not become accustomed to it.

Keep that goodness in your heart,
there's not a lot left of it,
in this world.

(To twelve-year-old me.)

They paid no attention to my progress.
So I pay no attention to their praise.

they only want what I have.

"Surely I've been at this depth before."

- Low day.

"We didn't have the same opportunities when we were young…"

This is something I have heard older people say (quite often). And-

"Why waste it?" was another.

But why push it if I,
or you, or they,
or we,
don't want it?

There is this pressure to seize something,
that we think we want it,
and we often feel ashamed for not taking the chance-
not because we actually desire it,
but only because we *could* have it, and not those before us…
even though we maybe didn't even want it in the first place.

Sometimes it's a chance that can change your life,
but if you well and truly don't need it,
let someone else take it.

Only you know what you really want.

My soul tends to leave my body
and wander off.

Nowhere in particular,
and I'm not sure how long for
until I come back around.

Head in the clouds (ii).

It's OK.
Anxiety is trying to get into my head, like the other times before.

"You won't do well."

"You'll fail," and-

"Why even attempt in the first place? What's the point if you're going to fail?"

-Try not to worry too much.

I’m grabbing a knife and stabbing
aimlessly at the darkness.

Hoping that somewhere-
anywhere-
the blade would rip or punch a hole
to let some light,

some hope-
back in.

-Pandemic.

I was never "Number One..."

I often feel like the odd one out.
for everyone around me always has someone else.

Someone who is better,
stronger,
funnier
braver,
fiercer,
smarter,
prettier,
than me.

I'll never be everyone's number one. I get that.
But I'm not number one for *no one* all the same.

As long as I am number one to *someone.* To anyone.
I should be happy.

There are many I cherish most dearly, more than my ten fingers can count for.
But I know I'm not their first,
their second,
third,
or even fourth choice.

I know there is someone who was lucky
enough to have them
before I did, and I wish we had met sooner.

When there's not much of my heart to go
around,
I must choose who gets a piece wisely.

Or else it'll only find its way back to me.

Broken.

The voice in my head has
been there forever.

I've only noticed
as of recently
how loud her
voice has
become.

Why haven't you talked about how you've been feeling?

I'm not doing it on purpose,
please don't think of it that way.

It's a little hard right now,
to find the right pattern
of words I need to say.

I'm not ignoring your messages.
I know you mean well.
Just give me some time,
that's all I ask…

~cos right now, I'm not exactly sure how I feel myself.

Brave the Storm ahead of you.

The clouds look frightening at the moment.

Who knows how the sea will react
as your boat nears the shade.
Who knows who will be in the boat with you
when the time comes.

Or if you must face it alone,

who will be there to greet you,
hug you,
love you.

When you come ashore.

"I feel like I talk too much already,
but I may not be able to say the right thing
the first time around."

-Jaw.

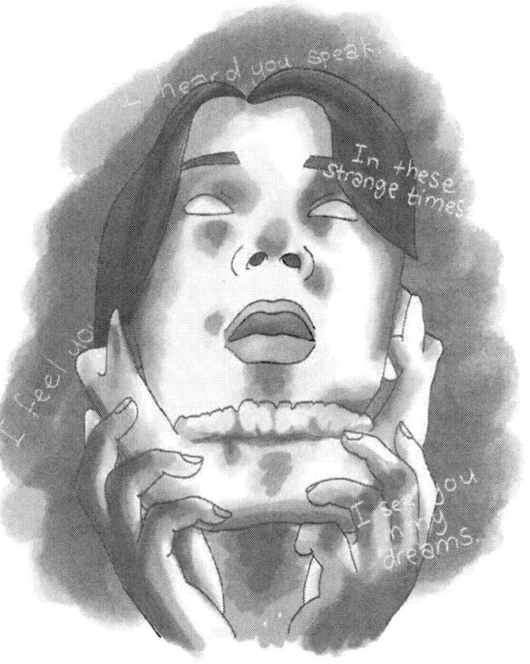

Haunted House

A derelict house,
where the floorboards creak and silence sings,
louder than my heart would usually allow.
Thunderclouds weren't constant; however,
clouds were always lurking.
No living souls were ever about this place.

A place I tend to visit time to time, not one you
can ever bring company.

A door handle that bared one set of fingerprints
would ever open,
to reveal glass lying like scattered petals along
the floor.

Not in a game of 'he loves me, loves me not'

I felt the pieces crack beneath my feet.
the soles of my shoes were my protection- but
to walk aimlessly, my head and heart remain
exposed.

The stairs beckoned me up,
A shaky hand on the peeling wood, I drag
myself along.
A pool of frames swam along the walls.

Each square was caked in dust,
some had glass cracked, others joined the rest
on the floor.

Others framed with golden flowers,
to grace the memory they had left behind.

The end of the hallway had a door.
There always an open invitation to go in.
For the thrill seekers who want in… you can't.
Please, with everything in me-
Keep. Out.

I haven't been brave enough to venture myself,
but I will... someday.

I walk through this haunted house
Where no one else can go,
I can't help it being exclusive,
But its somewhere close-

Where only *I* can roam.

-Procrastination-

I know it’s possible,
I know it can be done,
I just don’t understand why
I can’t bring myself to
get started.

Why can't the brain work like a USB drive?

To search the carefully organised folders,
relive the precious moments in video exactly
how they happened.

To never forget
the tender words that were spoken

To delete memories
that I never want to be reminded of again.

Strings

You hold one end,

I hold the other,

and we use them to find each other easily.

But there's changes in distance,
new networks,
that have our string entwined,
with many, many others.

It takes longer to find the time,
to untangle ourselves from the noise,
the lives we live in,
to find ourselves,

Reunited in the middle.

Feathers

It's a message from our dearly beloved,
the dearly departed-
That is left for us to find from time to time.

It may not be often,
but remember this:
when you need it most…

You will see a feather near-by.
It could mean absolutely anything,
but just know that;

They are always there.

I often wonder how you've been doing
nowadays.

What is it that gets you out of your bed in the
morning,
who you've been talking to lately,
what you're doing with your life.

But I can never call you to find out.

-we can never be friends again-

“Music is a *unique* Language”

Like poetry,
it’s melody, its rhythm
with words that can swim such a depth
within you,
and it stays.

I've seen passion die,
or barely recognised… because
apparently-
it's unfavourable to love something
so much,

*(where their eyes alight with a **spark,***
igniting their souls,
the joy,
*that makes their **world shine** a little bit*
brighter).

that the saddest of souls,
somehow find the pleasure to berate them.

-bully.

I only see you in my dreams,
It's been a long time since I heard you speak,
but I feel you.
In my heart.

Always.

The telephone

The view outside my bedroom window,
will need time getting used to.

But at 8.30pm.
Every night (mostly),
my work is done for the night.

The number is dialled.
I hear your voices.
The barking,
the normal chaos:

It brings me closer to home.

What is God's worst creation?

Of all the beautiful things that exist,
grow,
walk,
crawl,
blossom and bloom,
live,
and breathe…

it's us.

Look at the evidence- such greed for green
we destroy our home,
dragging all that's glorious down with it.

Of all the amazing things we can achieve- we
always turn to destruction.

WE are God's worst creation: you can't
change my mind.

Take those words apart,
chew them up,
grind them down,
if soft enough.

If they're tougher,
smash them up,
turn those damn shards into harmless stars,
a scattered alphabet in the sky,
instead of a dagger in hand.

-Reach Out-

Someone's out there for you.
Please reconsider.

Your pain may come to an end,
but someone else's…

-someone you love-

will begin.

it will stay with them,
for the rest of their life.

When you should be there-
talking,
smiling,
reminiscing,
Living- instead.

-you're not allowed to give up.

This is the year of graduations
unlike any other…

Not for me though-

At 21:

friends have graduated
in these strange times,
or they're nearly there…

At 21:

I'm starting fresh again,
A new chapter
and often feel like I am falling behind.

*My path of choice doesn't feel normal
sometimes.*

Look at what you can achieve,
when you let your heart get braver-
that little bit fiercer.

Despite what they think.

Those who are meant to be there?
They will be.

Those you thought would, but aren't?

That's okay too.

"No matter what,
it must teach nothing but love, compassion
and acceptance.
It should never condone violence and pain.

Only then will I convert."

-Religion.

The day you find yourself
hanging by a thread.

I'll be waiting.

Scrapping the ground in front of you,
Digging and clawing, until your nails split,
those long fingers bleed
as you beg for my help...

I'll be watching.

I'll sit on my hands to stop myself from
committing murder,
from pushing you over the edge...
and anticipate the moment you grow tired,
patiently waiting,
until you give up,
and let go.

- A letter to Anxiety.

Party

The drinks keep on pouring,
a game of Kings,
a round of Snap!
And Never Have I Ever...

Don’t stop the music,
put on that tune that’s been in our heads for
weeks,
keep the conversation going,
our mouths running,
allowing voices and laughter ring
through the air,
until the sun comes up.

Don’t let this atmosphere fizzle out...
I don’t want this party to end.

Only to be left with the reminder of how
lonely life was,
before you came along.

-to all my friends.

How to describe:
W-R-I-T-E-R-S Block

1. Like there's a **wall** between me and this piece of paper.

2. It's a **headache** that will not go away.

3. **Someone** has hold of my hand, refusing to let me pick up the pen.

4. All the ideas are there- in my head. **But my hand cannot transfer the words to paper.**

5. My head is as **blank** as a new word document.

6. Energy is there, but my **words get mixed up.**

7. Work gets in the way- there is **no motivation** left.

8. Words **fly away** before I can catch them in my butterfly net.

9. There is a **force field** that's blocking the way.

10. My body is too **tired.**

11. **Passion has hit another flat line…**

The day I had seen
the strongest of my friends and family
crumble,
mourning the loss of those dear to them,
was the day I understood
all it takes is one,
to break a million hearts.

When your friends can barely
stand on their own,
with the pressure, the strain,
their demons may pave the path to a darker
place,
or beckon them towards a darker depth
in a raging ocean
they may certainly drown in.

Be there.
Be that light they need to find their way
through the dark.
Or that raft that keeps them afloat.

-help them get to safety.

Twenty Things that I Love the Most-

1. The rain hammering against my window when I'm in bed at night, when I'm trying to sleep.
2. Treating myself to something after a busy school week.
3. Watching snow fall at the dead of night.
4. Seeing friends.
5. A few drinks out- or at home.
6. Staying up til 6am with family, drinking, playing games, laughing, and chatting about life.
7. Cuddled up next to Him.
8. Catching up with Meg, knowing life is blessing her well.
9. (a) Receiving letters during lockdown.
   (b) Responding to those letters.
10. Nightly calls to home.
11. Those nights where you could not sleep. Nothing is plaguing your mind, but there isn't anything to really look forward to. You just can't sleep… so you stay up to watch the sunrise in the summertime.
12. A cup of hot chocolate.
13. A song you used to love appearing on shuffle.
14. Dancing your ass off.
15. Reminiscing old memories through videos and photos.
16. Inclusion.
17. Plotting my next project, my next adventure.

18. Love(ing someone- but loving yourself is just as important).

19. Work needs to be done… but that book you've been reading has you on edge, how could you put it down now?!

And finally,…

20. You- for existing, creating, chasing, dreaming, and believing.

Is it ambition,
to strive with my art, to share my
chronicles?

Is it admiration of their work,
that is my inspiration?

Is it jealously,
to yearn for the recognition they have
despite my lack of experience?

-yes, it's definitely jealousy-

It's all about those faces in the background.

Some are the main characters in your life story, or they are just the side characters. They may not be on every page, let alone every chapter.

But they were always there for you no matter what.

Since the day, your first chapter together started.

"Escape"

It's more than a rectangle of words
and pictures.

It's a door that opens up,
arms that welcome you,
hands that cover your ears.

A new world that shuts out the old one,
Not forever, but for a little while.

Sometimes that's all you need.

Pluviophile- (n) a lover of rain.

Call me weird or strange.

Peculiar is a better word maybe.
I find my peace of mind.

On days where I'm in no rush to go anywhere,
To watch the rain hammer against my window.
I journal my thoughts in the grey haze.

Knowing the worries of yesterday
that hung over this house
can wash off
and go down the drain…

I feel grounded.

There is nothing like reading the works
of someone who has walked a mile in the
reader's shoes.

Even in the loneliest of experiences,
it's amazing how a few words
can be like a hand on your shoulder.
A gentle whisper-

"It's okay, I've been there too."

-are powerful enough to keep a heart alive.

The Devil is afraid of Losing

Why do you think he's keeping you close by?
Maybe, he keeps you in his pocket-
why must you stay in the dark?

He was everything you could possibly have
wanted:
but he was that friend your folks would warn
you about,
that partner your friends didn't favour,
that very creature that sucks the goodness
right out of you
if allowed.

But why is he afraid of losing?
There's this niggling feeling at the back of his
head,
a notion that he must try with everything
in his power to make you stay.

Knowing full well that he may crumble if
you leave him,
            her,
            them.

leave it behind, before you get burned.

"I am normal, I am beautiful,
natural.
I am yours,
please accept me."

-My body.

Funhouse Mirror

Laughter of the innocent young, pulling
funny faces,
To match the funny shapes.

Tall and lean, sucked in and wide-eyed
Short and stumpy, puffed out cheeks,
the parents laugh and join.

So many universes to see, marvel
and giggle at,
but one of them stopped.

Now, the memory still within my mind,
I notice the way my eyes reflect
How my pupils darken,
Almost saddened.

As I bend and twist my flaws
out of proportion
Snipped and starved
into perfection.

Once in a blue moon,
I may see something good in me,
But not always, like the rest.

Just like they can't see what goes on
in the organ that named itself.
This one isn't a funhouse mirror.

And nor is it found with others,
As I poke and prod,
Tears outlining those hollow cheeks…

"A mirror can't show the true beauty of a person"…
It is in the dark mind what I perceive..
what such beauty means to me.

She's become my most honest friend.

I do not see the changes,
I could *never* lie to myself...
Believe me,
I've tried before.

To pinch, to prod, to stare for the longest time.
To try and go about my day without worrying...
There are good days,
I grow fond of those,
Dreaming-

no, *wishing*
they would last forever...

Good things come to those who wait...

But others just don't get it,
unless their closest friend,
Is their own reflection.

The Garden

My eyes fell to the mercy of the garden.
Everything is peaceful with their own kind,
I watch each group and see all I need.

The roses stand out first; tall and elegant.
I dare not touch or compliment them,
As they bear thorns,
And already acknowledge their beauty.

Those cupid arrow orchids:
Notice me, they say!
Did Eros send you to earth?
Mysterious and beautiful, but I know little about
you.

Then I see the daisies and snowdrops,
Quiet and shy.
But they seek none of their achieved attention.
They welcome all happily, even the roses.

The temptation to send the Gardener one request.

"Please add another spoon of their beauty,
to a world in need of healing."

Is indeed strong and true.
I must stay with the daisies and snowdrops,
and make their army strong.
I hope others can fill the vacant spaces too.

I Will Wait

I'm not entirely sure when it all began,
Somewhere down this jagged line…
somehow,
We stopped being friends.
You deny the accusations, but you're not feeling the absence like I am.

Every impulsive thought that passes your eyes, every action you have done to harm yourself, has harmed me too.
I feel the pain, the confusion,
the starvation that we're putting ourselves through,

but you don't seem to bat an eyelid.
You solider on like there's nothing wrong with
you- with *us*.
I try to shield you from the danger.
Earlier nights, healthier habits, they develop eventually, right?

But your obsessions grew,
Presently, not as toxic as people would envision. You didn't let it show, but you were almost feeding on their comments.

You were raised higher than this! There is no place for the weaker links,
Let us make them vanquish entirely.

That’s what it was all about; you had
yourself on the highest pedestal for the
longest time.

Alas, even stone crumbles to dust…
But I won't lose my faith, even though it
seems you can't find yours.
Be still, this aching heart of ours.
I will watch you from afar,
and rejoice day by day, as you start over,
and learn to love yourself again.

Until you're ready, my friend
You'll find me at the mirror.

Bathroom Mirror

The steam of the shower was always
welcoming.
Standing under the waterfall, lapping in the
comfort it gives her, it was almost too warm
to leave....

Her phone lays beneath the window, hollow
and silent, while she stands before the
mirror.
Fogged up by the mist that flowed within the
room,
the window was open; the one at fault.

She inspects the outside world briefly;
Beyond the barrier, the air hangs low, a
black veil, once open.

Resealed, she resumes. Before thine eyes,
she is shielded by her own reflection. What
awaits in view?

A being so ghastly,
must it be gone by dawn?
A witch so twisted,
she poses a threat?

A patterned hand is out to touch the glass-
inhale,
exhale- swipe left.

Nothing of the sort.

Her modesty protected by her towel.
Shoulders poking the spaces awkwardly, the
chill crawls beneath the door.

Swipe right- her lips. Nude, exposed- no
vowels or song,
From a curved smile that could light up the
room, it lays domain- a flat line.

Left again- the eyes, weighed by black
sacks, those forget-me-nots,
cat-like and swollen- dark lush lashes sweep
the air with every blink.

Everything she used to be, cries out for its
return to the spotlight;
for its release from its dark cavern....
gone girl.

Stretch-Marks

I'm not sure when they first appeared,
these claw like marks-
pale streaks on my legs-
                    between them
                     hugging me,
                  just under the hips.

Will they ever go away?
They haven't made their move yet,
nor have I tried to get rid of them.

Maybe,
For however long,
they've inked themselves into my skin,
another feature of natural beauty,
embedded,
like the roots of a mighty tree,
into its soil,
to grow.

Skin

Your skin fits you like a glove.
It suits you well.

But it hurts my heart to see you hate it so,
when something so unique was designed for
you…

and you want it to be swapped for something
lighter,
something darker,
with freckles,
without freckles,
something that isn't you.

I love it on your person.

Please,
for me,
wear it proudly- it's your flag.
It's your canvas, so get creative.

Add some colour if you like.
Imprint every piece of work that describes no
one else,
but you.

Characters in my stories
aren't always their own person.

Sometimes they're everything
I don't or can't find in me...

Bravery, Beauty, Leadership, Wildness,
Strength, Self-Control, Confidence...

But you won't find me in the spotlight.
I don't like being the centre of attention.

-side character.

You preach kindness,
"All bodies are beautiful"
"be yourself".
"you're perfect just the way you are."

....

Yet when someone is nothing
but themselves, happy and comfortable in
their own skin.

They're strange and treated as such.
As if its bold to be happy,
That it's not okay...

being yourself is courageous,
don't lose it: that shit is rare to find.

Beautiful

Don't try to live up to society's
expectations.

who had the right to say what I can or can't
do?

with **my** hair?
or **my** body?
I wear on my own skin,
I can't tell anyone else
to wear theirs
the way I expect them to do.

I shouldn't expect them to do anything for
the sake
of keeping me happy.

Hell, if it were my way-
Everybody- and I mean *every body*
will walk the runway.

All vibrant and beautiful.
We celebrate our flaws,
because they make us unique,
from the crowd
we are expected to follow.

I have my days.

There are days I love the way I look, other days I don't… and as of late I have let myself go: I don't look after myself.

I sometimes think my legs are too big, and my stomach is sluggish.
my skin is not smooth and clean. I am not beautiful.

"There's nothing wrong with you." He told me.

I don't feel that way; and I don't think I have for a while- I just don't see it.

Here's to hoping this feeling goes away soon.

It has gotten to the point where,
my eyes still burn from all the tears,
but my body is numb.

my head is muddled,
staring blankly at my notes.

Stuff needs to be done,
deadlines need to be met,
but I can't bring myself to do anything about it.

-burnout.

Filters hide the blemishes.

They change my eyes,
brighten my hair…
thin my face,
chisel away the undesirable,
in all the right places.

They hide my flaws,
and make me something I'm not…

-perfect.

My skin turns marble in the cold
yet I don't freeze.

You can try,
but you can't take it away
and make me into something new...
something that isn't me.

I'm my own perfect sculpture.

“Do you really not see it?”

Do you not see your worth?
Do you not see the fire you set off
every time you walk into a room?

Do you not see…

Everyone who loves you,
and forget the ones who did once upon a
time…
(why should they matter now?)

You have yet to see the power
your presence has in this world,
or what it will become.

Do you *really* not see it…

Or are you afraid to look?

I regret not wearing that Navy blue dress...

For my graduation in 2017.
It was light, breezy,
off the shoulder,
all I needed was shoes to match.

I tried it on in the shop,
and my friend told me it was beautiful.

"Buy it," she said.
I watched myself in the mirror,

-thoughts pending...-

"No." she asked me why. "I need to explore
my options." I say.

In reality, I loved it.
I truly did.

The only problem was that
the worst side of me,
told me that it was pretty; indeed,
but would look better on someone else.
Anyone else-
                    but me.

I could see parts of me poking out in all the
wrong places,
which I never deemed natural.

Others may not see it,
but they can’t see through my lenses.

Yes,
now I regret not wearing the navy-blue dress
at my graduation.

I wish that voice in my head would just go away.

The more you poke and prod
searching for what you don't have,
or wish you had,
and hate yourself for it,
you will fail to see the good qualities about
yourself.

Your day will come;
The day you pick up your brush,
you will gather your broken parts,
and bring them back together in gold,
and see the beauty in what
you couldn't bear to look at,
shimmer.

- **the art of *Kintsugi**

***Kintsugi is the Japanese art of piecing broken parts of pottery back together with gold.**

Beauty must never be defined,
or singled down,
to one particular
standard.

- Let there be more than one type.

"The prettiest people have it worse."

The prettiest eyes have shed tears, to the point they were stained red.

The purest hearts have been robbed of their innocence.

The kindest of souls have been broken, ripped and torn apart into little pieces...

The strongest of bodies were weak once upon a time. They had been battered, bruised, and cut, and brought to their knees...

Even the most creative or smartest of minds have battled their demons. almost willing to give up.

However.

Those eyes were wiped dry.
Those souls still show grace and kindness, when they had every right to be angry.

Those hearts have put themselves back together.
Those bodies slowly, but surely, got back up onto their feet.

Those minds are still fighting, and are closer to victory.

If one of these apply to you-

It's you- you're are one of the prettiest people.

"This head of yours is too heavy to
carry.
Untwist the top and take out some of
those thoughts- share them, you must!
You'll feel a lot better-

As will I."

-Shoulders.

Fragile Case

She's put on display in that beautiful glass
case,
lace it in gold,
down her in flowers and gems.

Maybe being inside it makes her all
the prettier,
the more special,
the rarest jewel in the crown.

Put her on the highest pedestal,
to ensure no one else can get her.

"Don't leave the box."
"You must stay safe."
"This is the only thing keeping you safe."

Do they not know that glass can shatter?

She has every right to be free,
but the glass will not protect her.
She isn't safe,
with the way the world is right now.
(if it ever had been in the first place).

Your door is always open.

Even in these strange times.

On my days out, I can't count how many
times I've walked past your door
(one of many, I may add).

I'm not sure why I stopped talking to you.
I used to come to your house every week,
accompanied by my grandmother.

It must break her heart that none of us
ever come to see you.

Despite this, you have never shut us out.
The invite is always there.
A visit must be on the cards soon,
I must let you know how I am doing
nowadays.

I'm sure you've seen me around
but have yet to hear my progress
from my own lips.

this is God's house.

“Straight Pride”

Of all things,
we will never have the privilege
to make this our own.

We’re simply not entitled to it.

We have celebrated our love
from the very start with no judgement,
no fear, discrimination or hate.

We must continue to fight for everyone
else’s basic right to love,
to exist as their beautiful selves,
and comfort them during their struggles.

We will support them when others won’t,
and celebrate their victories.

Rain

Its mighty power is unveiled,
when it forms our rivers,
an element of Mother Nature,
that got us in our welly boots,
in simpler times.

All the same, while bringing happiness,
it brings devastation to others,
going from drizzle to heavy bullets,
From wet roads to flooded fears,
the black cape not far behind over-fed drains.
For me it's strange…

Hearing the tears hammer against my
window,
tsh tsh tsh tsh
When the suffering are in desperate need,
But instead lay to rest in the cold.

While the angels express their sorrows,
to those in our desolate streets tonight.
As I remain safe on a stormy night,
I count the many blessings that I take for
granted:

My country and my level of wealth, feeling
selfish,
In my sturdy home.

Sabaism

Taking the time to step away from the
digital bug
will do me the world of good.

In fact,
I would love nothing more
than to jump into a car,
and whisk off to an open field,
with no streetlights, no civilisation-
just to sit in the grass and watch the stars for
a little while.

They have sat back and watched everything
unfold before us,
since the beginning of time,
and had always been there,
even if we couldn't see them…

But when was the last time, we took a
moment to admire them?

(the worship of stars)

Attention

Women were not put on this earth for the pleasure
or benefit
of man.

Sweetie,
Don't think you can change the devil himself,
when it's not your job to do it.

If the devil could change his ways
and fix his errors,
surely God would've had enough power
to make him do so before.

If God can't change the devil,
what has you convinced that
you can?

"Why does it matter to you?"

What people wear,
what people do in their own home,
who holds their hand,
or sleeps in their bed,
what they do for a living,
how they express themselves,
what they do with their own bodies…

if it doesn't affect you?

-it's not that hard to mind your own business.

Mauerbauertraurigkeit

I am loved,
I am wanted,
I am alive.
I. Am. Important…

To everyone who loves me,
I'm sorry if you are sometimes met,
with a brick wall between us.

I'll take the blame…

I allowed my insecurities in once more.

More. Then. Once.

- **"wall builder sorrow".**

There's more than one way to talk to God-
to the Gods-
to Allah-
to who you believe in.
Don't let TV, the words on the street,
or distasteful propaganda hinder your love
for prayer.

(If you choose to believe any at all- that's okay too).

If it brings you comfort, keep that close to
your heart.
Pray to them.
Sing to them.
Read the parchment,
Light a candle,
Celebrate your beliefs.

As long as you don't allow it to alter your
beliefs as the one and only.
One may be enough for you, but others are
entitled to their own.

-Remember, there is more than one God; there is more than one religion.

Window Pain

Reaching out for your hand, and you do the same,
our fingertips barely caress one another.

There's glass in the way of our connection.
A screen that wasn't the only thing that kept us apart,
you were across the pond, not too far away,
but we were, in a sense, neighbours.

Not romantic, but friends- I never saw it any other way. One day, you knocked. You *needed* me, you said it yourself.

"The demons are coming out to play.
Save me. Before its too late."

I was your only hope.

You stepped back as I kicked, punched, and kicked some more- hammering my fists like I was playing a drum.

My knuckles are bleeding, but no damage was done to the shield,
Before you broke the silence.

"It was a joke."

There were no demons... danger wasn't coming for you; it was only a trick to ensure that I would never leave.

I kept away from the glass after that, despite your pleas and promises to break the glass and walk the shards for my forgiveness until you bled...

Until slowly, but surely, I rebuilt that barrier.

This time, I painted it black. You can't see me anymore.

You have knocked on the glass once or twice, but soon enough, I never heard from you again.

It's safer this way.

"All Lives Matter"?

This is what you told me, right?
Maybe it wasn't you, sorry for the
assumption- but someone's been saying it,
Done by tongue and teeth, or it was on their
story.

And I apologise again- all lives don't matter.

If they did,
Our brothers and sisters of colour,
would not be fighting for their rights as men,
woman,
gay, straight, cis, trans, non-binary,
teachers, nurses, doctors, parents, children...
human beings.

So tell me again-
"do all lives **really** matter?"

Try telling all the voices that were silenced
in the hands of hate,
that their lives always mattered...

When there are riots, shootings, war,
famine... **do they all really matter?**
until all is equal in respect, shelter, security,
and safe from danger...

All lives don't matter.

I'm the one in charge of
the reins of my horse.

No one should ever have that
power over
me.

I may have let them before,
but never again.

I may have fallen once or twice,
but that's all part of
learning how to ride and
tame a wild horse
that lived
in me.

Unknown

An irritating buzz of a silent radio station,
she knits in front of the window,
the silken curtains barely caressing her
sides.
A single notation waved around her ears,
but not from the radio.
She slowly stood to the noise.
A mist flowed around the room,
ran through the wisps of her platinum locks,
a silhouette, a dainty being, a sorrowful
song,
tip-toed fairy-like around the room,
Here it be her private show.

There she patiently waited for the song to
finish,
to interrogate and ask for a reason,
for her presence.
Once the haunting melody had vanished,
Into the air around them,
The eyes open, face well defined.
A gasp as the mist goes too,
she is face to face with a mirror.
A woman,
once flamboyant in a by gone era,
now an arrogant hag,
she be dwarfish,
downed in a flowing gown and cardie,
aged and brittle boned.

We're all capable of doing
bad things.

It doesn't matter who you are,
the colour of your skin,
or where you come from.

But there is the select few,
a handful-
that act on those dark intentions.

Don't mix it up with bravery.

You're barely human.

-Monster.

You took me by surprise
when you asked me for my opinion.
I waited for a moment,
before I could find the words
to put in the right pattern.

I could honestly
cry so hard
because never
have I ever
felt like my
opinion ever
ever…

-mattered.

"Eating isn't the very thing that's
feeding me, so don't starve yourself
in a desperate attempt to kill me.

It's not going to work."

-Anxiety.

All the stress is washed away,
almost cruelly as the sponge
scrapes my skin.

Bubbles hug every curve
as the mist hangs over,
soft music plays,
as my thoughts, my burdens of the week,
rinses off.

Maybe they'll return Monday morning.

-Self care.

Maybe I was just stubborn.
It felt like forever since then.
I took it upon myself
(it was two weeks after the fact),
to tell my school Chaplin.

"I don't need her anymore. I'm only wasting her time.
I'm okay now."

He was stubborn too.
A gentle smile before he shook his head…
"Believe me, it's too soon."

"I swear I'm okay- I'll be okay."

"Please give yourself more time."

I didn't want to,
but maybe I was a people-pleaser,
because I agreed.

It took some time to realize,
Indeed. It was for me.

-Therapy Sessions.

"In an ideal world…"

Everyone would be free.
they would be happy,
well,
safe,
themselves.

No war, just peace.
No fright, or harm.
a world where every child has a home,
where every body is beautiful,
there is no judgement or hate.

There would be nothing but love and compassion,
and everyone is equal.

…

…

In an ideal world.

"This notebook only has so much paper."

- *There's limited space*
  for the infinite thoughts
  that go on in my head.

If Heaven Had a Phone Number

I hope there's a line of people waiting at the other end for me.

It doesn't have to last forever...
As long as I get to say what needs to be said,
or even a simple "hello" or "goodbye",
as I didn't have a chance to before.

"Another year"

Another year of uncertainty,
another one of possibly failing,
of worry and doubt.

That niggling feeling that it
won't be possible to succeed,
the temptation to stay in bed.

Hang in there little love,
it'll work out in the end.

I(a)m-possible

Crazy how some words come out of
someone else's mouth,
and I keep note of them.

-Inspiration.

Not everyone has water up to their toes

If you can swim, keep in mind not
everyone can keep their head above the
waves.

Some of us have gone under and get
back up again.
Then there are those who never
resurface,
or fight the current that
took them down.

Don't let it be every
person for
themselves.

Make sure you toss a
ring,
and save
someone
from going under.

The day you arrive,
will be the one I
cherish the most.
(to my future children).

What will I come up with tomorrow?

- anticipation.

Roses

I am a rose, red and elegant,
Her favourite type.
In a big garden, I'm not alone,
One big bush, close and together always.

There is more like me....
It's rare we grow apart.
In winter we are together to sleep,
With peace when we awake.

In the warm Spring.
We're not alone in the garden....
Bluebells, white daisies, and yellow Busy-
Lizzies,
Sit together far below happily.

This I don't ever understand!
They're different to me, red nor elegant,
Yet they dance in harmony....

In their light afar, from my reaches,
We are pampered with attention,
And they dance and, sway sweetly alike,
I envy, I want to be there…

But I can't,
Not with my thorns.

The Divide in the Road

Wonder, wonder, wonder,
my mind and soul will carelessly wander,
of the unknown that is to come.

I understand the road can go
more than two ways:
up down, left right,
Good or bad,
the way I'd like it to,
or the way I don't.

For some they have an idea of their
direction,
they may already be well on their way.
They could be sunk, or stepping down,
letting it brew,
or became stranded on the curb…

While others, like me,
Just walk in the middle of the lanes,
the thinning divide in the never-ending road,
Waiting for fate to set the pieces,
and holding back for the right car to thumb
to,
for that destined hitch.

Goblin in the Garden

Only up to my knee,
He sits by the flowers
On either side of him,
Covered with gentle moss,
As he guards the plants,
Still in silence all the while
With pride.

A small little statue,
Not even a garden gnome!

But a goblin.

Born with his high head,
And ugly face,
He sits snugly in the muck,
Of my grandmother's garden,
comfy.

Would you call it pride?
His twisted face doesn't show
As I used to sit by him,
And I joined him in the serenity.

While looking at the flowers,
I realise that he was alone,
No other statues were there.

Until the Saturday before Easter,

When I was sixteen,
A white eagle statue appeared,
Flying from the Druids Chair,
And a crucifix for my brothers and I.
My dad just shook his head and said:

"These damn symbols!"

Stranger (i)

"Hello again-
I've seen you around before..."

I wait for a response,
but you walk right past me.
Wait-
you hesitate, just briefly,
before you glance at me.

Those eyes I used to gaze into:
a familiar face? Yes-
I recognise you.
But do I *know* you?
I did...
But not anymore.

So long ago we would laugh together,
that contagious laugh,
a by-gone memory.
You used to know me,
and I to you,
but life set us on different paths.

-when friends become strangers.

The House Rests

Every morning there is the
usual hustle and bustle.

Kettle boiling
microwave going,
Dog's barking,
Hoover running,
machines washing, drying, whirling
it feels like the house is a city of its own,
that never sleeps.

That is…
Until the dead of night,
when every soul is sleeping in their beds,
the dog wakes up now and then to check on
the other occupants,
before settling back down in the warmth.

Not a single sound is heard within this
dwelling,
and ***this*** is the only time,
that this house-
any house-
is finally
at rest.

I’m always searching for ways to
better myself:
better grades,
better body,
a higher self-worth.

But no matter what-
where I go-
who I go to-
or how much I try to improve,
I often feel broken with exhaustion.

Do you get this too?

-I’m pushing the limits.

Stranger (ii)

To think we were all together once upon a
time.

In one room, so many faces, so many chairs.
all eyes are on the board, in our books or at
each other.

Memories dance inside my head:
the stuff said
things that were done
the laughs that we've had.

That was only a few years ago.

How quick time does fly?
it seems like a lifetime,
all of us in the same room.
Friends, enemies, acquaintances.
(whether the past or present plurals apply).

All now where life has decided to take us,
even if some of us are still on the road.
Different streets.

We're practically strangers.

"Glass child"

"I don't want to be held,
or carried like I am-
was-
this small fragile thing."

"Normality was the only thing I needed to
remain grounded…"

"I couldn't let myself crumble.
I don't favour the idea that I was weak,
going through such a troubling time."

You never truly get over it,
but the heart-breaking reality is:
You grow to accept it.

Loss.

-There is only so much I can do-

Please hear me when I say so.
I listen when I can,
when it seems like no one else will.

I know that not everything is working out
the way you want it to,
that the whole world is against you,
and you're the only one backed up against
the wall.

But like you,
I am only human,
I get so tired and frustrated,
but please be patient with me.

I would give anything to make you feel safe
and happy.

But it's not always that easy,
and it breaks my heart.

Are you with me?

I'm not sure why I am writing this-
I don't even know who this is for
(if for anyone at all).

Are you with me?

In this strange, complicated journey,
with all the twists and turns imaginable?

Are you with me?

I don't want to be in this alone-
We're "in this together" right?
To have each other's backs,
to hold hands,
to wipe away the tears
that outlined our cheeks with mascara
more times then I can count?

Here we stand at the crossroads,
not sure where they can take us,
let alone what awaits for us at the other end.
The red light has moved to Amber,
who knows when it'll go green.

....

Will you go with me?

"There was so much uncertainty and excitement,
in the times I forced myself to keep quiet…
but I'm calm now."

-My heart.

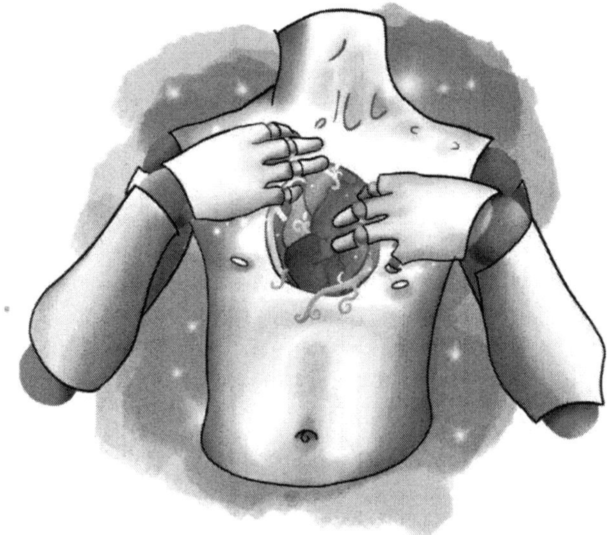

I pushed you away,
in fear of you hurting me,
like the one before,
but no matter what length I kept you at,
you stayed.

- Mended by you.

“If you want to grow,
you have to move away
from the soils where
nothing grows from.”

Grow where you can be supported and loved.

I don't regret what we shared…

Or the time we spent together
no matter who we were:

Friends or Lovers
or even by-gone enemies.

No matter what drove us apart
I'm still grateful for what we did had
or what you had taught me to look for in the future.

Those lessons of life I have carried with me
since our final chapter ended,
and led me to start more with someone else
whom I simply cannot live without.

I was happy with what we had shared,
even though it just wasn't meant to be.

I'm okay with that now.

I am grateful that
most nights I am granted peace
without the demons whispering in my ear.

However,
there are nights I lay awake:
no particular reason why.

My heart feels alive,
My brain stimulated to stay awake
too excited to close my eyes,
the rare time I don't seek rest.

Instead, I just sit in the dark
and think of all things I'm grateful for,
pondering what's next in store,
as I wait for the sun to grace me with
his presence,
and wake up the sleepy souls around me.

He announces a new day,
beckoning me to chase it.

- **I'm wide awake.**

No one has ever apologised
for making you “a total bitch”
or “a heartless wagon”.

You were hurt,
that heart has been hung out to dry too many
times before.
While you supposed better-half walks away.

You have been pushed into the corner,
afraid to talk back when
everyone has been looking down on you.

Then one day,
you fight back,
cut strings,
or even simply said “no”.

And suddenly you’re the worst person in the
world.

-funny how the world works these days.

I lay in pieces,
like a complicated jigsaw puzzle.
No one has tried to put me together.

Until you came along.

It took some time, and I may have pulled
myself apart,
but you never gave up.

-you're the only one who stayed-

I found love when I least expected it.

This heart of mine was still on the mend,
and when I thought it wasn't ready to love
again
(for some time I used to think).

The glue that brought it back together
was mentioned,
was spoken to,
was closer than I ever imagined.

The best kind of love.

All it takes is a single
act of betrayal
before the taste of trust
is foreign to my tongue.

-trust is the rarest honey
a bee can harvest-

"He hurt you."
A conversation with my boyfriend.

I can't help but feel that you wished to have
been there sooner,
to save my heart before it ever got broken.

"It's my job to look after you, and to love
you."

Yes,
it is now- and had been since we got
together.
But I don't want you to feel this burden.
You're not responsible for the heartache I
felt,
before you.

The Room with the Red Door

The room was cold and unkept,
the windows locked with drawn curtains.
I have been summoned here.

Two soft chairs come into view
as the door shut and bolted behind me.

Pray that I can get out again-
I take the empty seat.

There I am- aged 15
in my school uniform, and a little shaken up.

Her little white hands
take mine- they are cold to the touch.

Here came the questions.
"What happens next?"
"Where am I now?"
"Why did this happen to me?"

The uncertainty in her voice made the room
a little colder.
Our hands were still entwined, but I give her
a gentle squeeze to keep her grounded.

"It's okay now." I told her. "There has been
a lot of changes, like the autumn leaves- but
better things are coming your way."

"How do you know?" She asked, and the room gets warmer as I pulled her into a hug, a gentle whisper passing my lips.

"I'm the proof you made it."

We all have this friend...

We have a love/hate relationship.
Who is this, you ask?
Sometimes they go by the name of Fate,
Intention,
Purpose,
or even Fortune.

But I call mine Destiny.
Whether she means to or not,
she has ruined my life.

Rejection,
Heartache,
Anguish,
Confusion,
Sadness,
Disappointment...

At every twist, I ask “why?”
There's no comforting hand,
but she smiles at me.
“I have to let you hurt,” she tells me every time.

-because better things are coming.

I love seeing you in your element…

There is nothing more comforting than to
see you thrive in what you love.

A head in a book,
A song on your tongue.
Cooking up a storm,
Dancing to your own rhythm.
Painting a picture worth every feeling
of your vibrant being.

Writing, sharing your stories, your battles,
despite those who tell you not to.

8 : August : 2020

"Hold on,
Better things are coming,
I promise you.
Just you wait and see.
It will all work out."

-a message to the past.

Airport Anxiety

The airport felt too large,
my heart almost couldn't take it.

Almost.

Traveling Solo, Germany 2019.

Your jacket hangs under the stairs
and has done so
since the day my mother got her hands on it.

I found it last night
underneath all the other coats
almost frightened by
the sight of it.

Not because I didn't like it,
but because for a split second,
I thought you were still here,

- **Grandad Paddy**

I have never seen the sea so calm.

I've seen it furious many times before,
for something so beautiful,
but it was having a good day today.

Even when the Dart
would rattle behind me,
above me
caught my attention from time to time,
the water wasn't disturbed.

The waves were present,
but were gentle and welcoming
to anyone who ventured in
no matter how long they stayed.

It remained calm.

01:06:2021

“Keeping close contact,
But change it up a little,
Taking time out of your day, and tell me
how you’re doing,
how you’re coping in these strange times,
when your mouth fails to speak.”

-Letters.

The thing about music is that…

it is the most powerful thing in the world. It had such a way that it could cast a spell- a tidal wave of emotion,
without you asking it to.

Everyone has their own song that is kept close to their heart.

There are infinite songs out there that;

- Helped you fall in love.
- Had you heartbroken and missing people you didn't even know.
- Bring out that fire as you swept gracefully across the stage.
- Brought you to that happy place.
- It somehow turned back the hands of time, to that moment in history you wished you could've witnessed.
- It sets off that spark that inspires you
It sets off that spark that motivates you
the spark that brings out the beast,
that brings out the beauty,
that brings out the vulnerable,
the passionate
you.

"They never stopped
praying,
hoping,
wishing,
pushing,
and encouraging me,
when I was the one who felt like giving up."

~ Mam and Dad,
thank you <3

Time Capsule

One day,
sometime forward
I can look back;
at this collection of work,
my chronicles of
power
war,
love and hate
which will be history.
But one thing is for sure,
all that was felt-
Laughter,
Anguish,
tears-
will remain on these pages,
like a tattoo,
or a picture in a frame,
where the youthfulness will never grow old.

"Get out there already!"

All those words that dance in circles,
Deep inside your head,
Are eagerly waiting for you to grab that pen.

Opportunities are waiting for you out there,
with your book of rhymes,
chronicles of adventure,
with those anticipating your debut.

You don't know it yet my dear, but-

There are souls that grace this earth,
kicking their heels, waiting for your words
to appear,
to touch their hearts, and stick with them,
Like ink to paper.

Write your ideas,
your hopes,
your dreams,
your goals,
your wishes,
down.

Right now-

on a page, in a notebook,
anywhere…
as long as you can keep it safe.

Don't ever let them go,
or they will fly away,
from your reaches
like dandelion fluff in the wind.

Gold Dust

Have faith in that pixie dust-
something that's kept with me my whole
life.

no matter what pain or heartache
you have been through,
or have yet to dive into
head-first…

When it is time for change
just close your eyes and

believe.

Delivered

To the woman I have become:
I felt the need to write to you quickly,
please let me know if this gets to you.

My head has been an unwanted swarm of
perceptions,
the good, the bad, and the unknowing,
I need answers.

I haven't been informed on your
whereabouts...

Where are you now?
Are you home? Or is 'home' now elsewhere?
Across the pond? Across the street?

No one can tell me how you are.
(that or they choose not to....)
in your body, your mind, your soul.

The clouds are grey at the moment,
my reasons as of now are unclear.

Therefore, I pray for you that,
your skies are brighter and wider in your
opportunities to roam.

There has been no message, no warning,
on who is there, and who is not.

Who have you held onto for so long,
only to let go with a heavy heart?

It's unclear to see who threads about,
with a flower to put in my hand,
or knife to my back.

All in all, I hope you are:
Happy, healthy, confident,
singing, stable,
successful.... and at peace.
Sincerely,
The girl you used to be.

Until next time....

Acknowledgements

Words simply cannot express how I'm feeling right now. Its crazy to think that I always dreamed of publishing something- for a *long* time… and we're talking about since the age of seven or eight years old!

I had it in my head that I was going to be published by the time I was sixteen… and here we are, at age twenty-two, and I'm finally writing my acknowledgements at the end of my very first book… even if it is "just a load of poetry".

Maybe it was all worth the wait in the end- maybe I had nothing to share at the time, even though I kept trying to convince myself otherwise that I did!

Initially, I never thought I would drabble into poetry- the first one I ever wrote was at sixteen (not in this collection sadly), and a few more that soon followed. Some were quite personal to me, or gifts to friends, and some were just awful!

Anyways, there are a few people I'd like to thank.

To my Mam and Dad- thank you for never giving up on me, in anything I've done. You've showed nothing but encouragement and never-ending support. I am forever grateful.

To my brothers Felix and Dano- our house may be messy, but I wouldn't change you both for the world.

To my extended family- for all the laughter and tears we've shared over the years.

To my boyfriend Mark- for loving me, supporting me, and accepting all of me.

To my amazing illustrator, CJ- thank you for taking your talent and adding it to the pages. I will treasure them forever.

To Aoife, Enda, Chelsea, Rachel, Mark W, Danny Mc, David, Anne, Sophie C, Lochlainn, and Crego- you guys mean the world to me.

To Britta- you always had your head in a book, so here is one with your name in it!

To Lauren McCombe- a fellow author and dear friend who was so helpful in the process of making this book.

To Megan McDonald- for our by-gone school days where we would sit in English class, and you would read my **very** early work. I got around to making a book in the end!

To Megan "Eggy" Fitzgerald- thank you for helping me with the title!

And finally, to you, **my dearest reader.** I hope you found comfort in the pages- and know you are not alone in these feelings.

Thank you.

About the author

Born and raised in Dublin, reading and writing has always been part of Áine's life; her grandmother always made sure she had the latest books from her favourite authors growing up!

After graduating from Cabinteely Community School, and thanks to the current pandemic, Áine rediscovered a passion for writing poetry, and got her first book *In Motion* in the works.

Áine is now studying Nutrition and Health Science in Athlone, with a notebook and pen never too far away to write down her next idea...

You will find Áine on Instagram @thepenpiper and @itsanniem_22

About the illustrator

Clarissa-Jane Obongen, also known as CJ (or Ozma), is a young non-binary Irish digital artist. Recently graduating from University College Dublin with a BA Joint Honours in Art History and Irish Studies, they stream video games on Twitch as Ozma Chan in their spare time, as well as campaign stories for Dungeons and Dragons.

CJ has known Áine since secondary school and is very pleased to have the opportunity to make both their dreams a reality!

You can find CJ on Instagram @ozma.artngames

Printed in Poland
by Amazon Fulfillment
Poland Sp. z o.o., Wrocław

81095000R00098